Twelve voices were shouting in anger, and they were all alike. No question, now, what had happened to the faces of the pigs. The creatures outside looked from pig to man, and from man to pig, and from pig to man again; but already it was impossible to say which was which.

George Orwell
Animal Farm, 1944

 Extremely FOREWORD

The author of this volume has endeavoured to embody some of the results of his own experience and observation in society. He submits this work to the public, with the hope that the material contained in it may prove to be beneficial to others . . .

May I buy you a drink? You know, I've been watching you for quite some time from right over there in the corner.
What's that? No, I'm not with the Xerox convention.
They're over at the Peach Tree Towers aren't they?
It must be crawling with powder blue polyester in the Peach Pit Lounge tonight.

So, you're probably wondering what it is that I do for a living.
I'm a writer. I've been awake working for about 39 hours now.
I'm down here to unwind.
. . . . And, well . . . What I've been wanting to say is . . .
You're not my woman but you could be! . . .

(The drink! The drink! Buy her that drink you idiot! Be more forward! Chicks like this get plucked right out from under the perspiring little palms of the hesitant—you've seen it happen a thousand times!)

Really . . . I've been up all night writing for weeks—kinda lonely, you know—being a writer . . .

(Cut with the writer crap—she doesn't care! Tell her about the love accessories that you have at home! C'mon!)

. . . Do you like sexy books? . . . A lot of good articles . . .

(The pictures! Tell her about the pictures! Nobody reads anymore!)

. . . Of course, I don't care about the articles. Who does?
I'm more interested in what's going on in the pictures.
This may seem rather forward of me, but I would enjoy mimicking what they do in those pictures . . .
(With someone like you!)

. . . Yeah, with someone like you.

THE BEST OF PLAYBOAR

WRITTEN BY
THOMAS HAGEY

THE BEST OF PLAYBOAR is not licensed by or affiliated in any way with any existing magazine or publication. All names, products, addresses, phone numbers and identifying marks of any kind other than the information appearing on the masthead on page two is purely fictitious. Any similarity to real persons, firms, corporations or products is purely coincidental.

PRODUCTION AND EDITING:
Christopher Lowry
Mardie Weldon

ART DIRECTION AND DESIGN:
John Ormsby
Bob Wilcox

PHOTOGRAPHY: Stan Switalski, Bill Findlay, Chris Gosso, Steven DeNure, Jeff Carroll, J. Lloyd Hagey, Taffy's glasses by Anke Davids.

ILLUSTRATION: Shirley Al, Jim Brewster Kelvin Case, Anne Dunbar, Colin Hillcoat Ann Hunsberger, Kim LaFave, Barry E. Lavender, Chuck Nichols, David Prothero, Bob Suzuki, Tom Taylor, Murray Tonkin.

Cataloguing in Publication Data

Hagey, Thomas
    The best of Playboar
    ISBN 1-55209-060-4

1. Swine - Humour. 2 Playboy (Chicago, Ill.) – Parodies, imiations, etc. I. Title.

PN6231.S895H34 1996   C818'.5407   C96-931400-0

A FIREFLY BOOK

Published by Firefly Books Ltd. 1996

Firefly Books Ltd.
3680 Victoria Park Avenue
Willowdale, Ontario
Canada M2H 3K1

Published in the U.S. by
Firefly Books (U.S.) Inc.
P.O. Box 1338, Ellicott Station
Buffalo, New York 14205

Printed and bound in Canada

Dedicated to the memory of David Wayne

BENSON & HEDGEHOGS

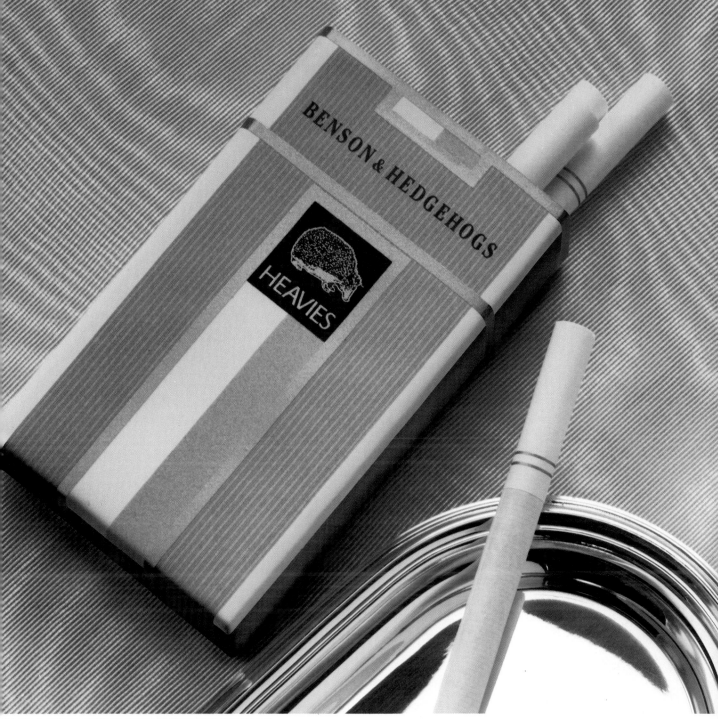

Heavies

10 megatons''tar'',' 10 megatons nicotine av. per cigarette FTC Report Dec.'84

6:45 pm... Humans grazing in a field near Austin Minnesota.

Hamtrack. We take more pigs to more places than all other railways combined.

CONTENTS

THANKS TO: The Hagey Family, Sunny Cedars Farm Ltd., Tracey Alexander, Barbara Allen, Marsha Boulton, Howard Burke, Cathy Cloud, Richard Cooper, Gary R. Dahl, Cindy Elizuk, Jeff Evensen, Nancy Finkle, Betty Gallander, Anthony J. Gilroy, Gordon Haight, Liz Gould Hawley, Willoughby House, Kathryn Irwin, Dr. Paulette Jolley, Arnold Nasco, Wayne Oakley, R. J. Robertson, Richard Sanders, James Shaw, Chris Singleton, Gary Shepherd, Glen Stemmler, Bob Wardrop, Ryan Yoshy, Zal Yanovsky, Alan Ramsay and Associates, Farm and Country Magazine, Tom Lewis/Contact Graphics, Slumpy Fulton, Slick Willy, and all other friends of Tom Hagey.

ACKNOWLEDGEMENTS: From ANIMAL FARM by George Orwell, copyright 1946 by Harcourt Brace Jovanovich, Inc.; renewed 1974 by Sonia Orwell. Reprinted by permission of the publisher. The Estate of the late Sonia Brownell Orwell and Secker and Warburg Ltd. The Observer for permission to reproduce "Pigs were targets in NATO exercise" by Ian Mather, published in the Toronto Globe and Mail, March 20, 1984. CP Wire service for permission to reproduce photographs.

INNERVIEW
WITH A. PIG

*O*ne of Hollywood's lesser known actors talks to PLAYBOAR about sex, losing movie parts to Richard Gere, Robert de Niro, and Dustin Hoffman, and what it was like to be Arnold Ziffle's stuntman.

PLAYBOAR: In all your films you play a pig. Why?

PIG: Because.

PLAYBOAR: Isn't there always a sense of the outlaw in your work?

PIG: Isn't there? I always thought there was. Oh! I see, you're asking me. Well, I played an outlaw pig in "Old Yeller" and in the "Thornbirds". I'm always killing people...Alright, so I'm an outlaw—big deal!

PLAYBOAR: What do you think of Meryl Streep?

PIG: I like her. I think she's a wonderful actress. I went to her house for dinner once—she wasn't home. I didn't want to get intimate, I just wanted to grab, maybe, coffee and truffles with her in that little cafe where she hung out, to glimpse her son Billy walking to school in Kramer vs. Kramer. I was almost in Kramer vs. Kramer.

PLAYBOAR: Kramer vs. Kramer?

PIG: Yeah! I auditioned for Dustin Hoffman's part—he beat me out. Too bad. They said I looked too much like a pig. They were right—I did.

PLAYBOAR: Do you compare yourself to Robert de Niro?

PIG: I'm not sure what you mean by that. I have long floppy ears—he doesn't. I'm a pig—he isn't. He was "Raging Bull"—I wasn't. I tried out for that part too. He beat me out. They said I looked too much like a pig. I asked them if they would consider changing the name of the film to "Raging Boar"—They wouldn't.

PLAYBOAR: You played Arnold Ziffle in "Green Acres" didn't you?

PIG: Yes, and no. I was Ziffle's stuntman. I was the guy who had to jump off the couch and turn the channel on the television. In the episodes where Arnold went to Hollywood, I was the one who had to risk my life getting on the Hooterville Cannonball—not Ziffle. I did anything that Arnold either flat-out refused to do or that he felt was too dangerous. That's what stuntmen get paid to do. I still get royalty cheques from "Green Acres".

PLAYBOAR: Do you find yourself attractive?

PIG: I'm not Richard Gere, but I'm not the Elephant Man either.

PLAYBOAR: Professionally, would you say that you're in the same league as Richard Gere?

PIG: Well, obviously Richard Gere has had a lot more successes than I have but he's accepted a lot of roles that I wouldn't have touched. I certainly feel that I'm as good as he is. I auditioned for his role in "American Gigolo". He got the part. They said they didn't care how well I claimed I could root—I still looked too much like a pig to them. I said that if they changed the name to the "American Pigolo" I'd be perfect. They didn't.

PLAYBOAR: Do you really think they felt that Gere was a better actor than you?

PIG: No. And I personally don't think he is. I'd like to see Richard Gere do "Arnold Ziffle goes to Hollywood". He tried out for the part but they said he

didn't look enough like a pig. I got the part—he didn't. The score's even.

PLAYBOAR: We aren't going to ask you this question.

PIG: Okay. That's fine with me.

PLAYBOAR: How did you become interested in acting?

PIG: I fell into it in high school. Then, much to my surprise, I landed a roll as a wild pig with rabies in the film "Old Yeller". I tried out for a minor part in "Pygmaleon" (My Fair Lady) but they said I looked too much like Rex Harrison.

PLAYBOAR: That's a bit of a switch, eh?

PIG: Yes, and a bit of a compliment to Rex.

PLAYBOAR: Do you have groupies?

PIG: Hell no! Why, do I have something growing off my lip?

PLAYBOAR: No...no, Groupies! Do you have groupies?

PIG: Yes, I suppose so. I don't think it's so much that they want to take me to bed, I think it's more that they want to say that they know me.

PLAYBOAR: You're Catholic. What do you think about the Catholic Church?

PIG: The first thing that comes to mind is collection plate. The second thing that comes to mind is men and women dressed in funny outfits, abstaining from intercourse. I can handle collection plate. However, abstaining from intercourse is sheer lunacy. Then again, abstinence makes the heart grow stronger. Narf, narf, narf.

PLAYBOAR: When you were single did you find it easy to get women?

PIG: It wasn't easy. It was never easy! They'd always say, "You're not like all the other boys are you?" I got my fair share though. Sooner or later everyone has to lie down or go to sleep!

PLAYBOAR: Didn't you find that that approach to sex was kind of..., kind of...

PIG: Empty? Is that the word you're looking for? Empty? Yes, but I didn't feel alone. Forty-nine per cent of Americans do the same thing to each other every night. "Once again to the diaphragm, only this time could we show just a little more feeling?"

PLAYBOAR: Do you feel that you were type-cast as Arnold the pig?

PIG: No! But I got a lot of tail being mistaken for Arnold. Him and me look a fair bit alike in the dark. But then, we all do. There is a lot of pig in me that still must come out and I'm anxiously waiting for the right script to come along; I'm optimistic that it will. I think I've got a hidden talent for sex and violence. I can see me doing roles like Dirty Harry, Buford Pusser, James Bond—that kind of thing.

 # WHAT SORT OF HAM READS PLAYBOAR?

He buys it because he likes to read the pictures. He's nobody's fool and isn't at all like the rest of them. He buys champagne by the case and wants to marry a female with a G-spot. Yes... That's what sort of ham reads Playboar.

Sometimes it takes a good smack-up to bring family and friends closer together.

Those Amazing LITTERMATES

Littermates say the darndest things, don't they? We think so. And we're proud of them. Each month in our magazine, we ask our former Littermates to answer a simple question. We've taken the best answers from a variety of subjects, over a number of issues, and compiled them here for your enjoyment. We think you'll be amazed at just how smart these girls really are.

We asked Jodi Monaham:

How did you learn about sex?

I learned about sex at and after school. My parents didn't tell me anything. The subject just wasn't encouraged. My parents did however give me a book when I turned seven months old entitled Molly's Babies. It was about a young Guinea Pig named Molly, who never listened to her parents and her parents never listened to her. Anyway, Molly liked to go down to the back of the property beyond the garden with friends to nibble. Then one day she met Frank the Rabbit. Frank, like his name, was very direct. They would often meet alone to nibble. Oh, how they loved to nibble! Then a change took place. This change put a lot of strain on the relationship. The nibblings gave way to quibblings and then there were siblings – It all ended on a very unhappy note and I could not, for the life of me, figure out what the story had to do with real pigs having sex.

I first heard about real sex in my sex education class in high school. It wasn't until after school that I got experience in the field.

I met this guy. Strangely enough his name was Frank. On our very first date we drove far out into the country to play this game of his. He called it, "Let's see if we can guess how many miles this place is from town." I guessed 30 miles, Frank guessed that it was probably closer to 50. "Now let's check," he said. "You walk and I'll keep pace in the car. Or we could play another game I know." That was that. I figured anything, even sex, had to be more fun than a fifty-mile walk and I'm sure that it is. After all, I get excited about having sex all the time. I never get excited over the thought of a fifty-mile walk – at least not in these shoes.

We asked Ursowla Hamdress:

Is there anything about boars or the way boars live that you envy?

Nice try Playboar. If you think I'm going to fall into your neat little trap, forget it! I don't need to be accused of weiner envy and that's exactly what would happen. I love being a sow and if you want to know the truth, I don't envy boars at all. That's my answer.

We asked Melissa Muckdonald:

Have you ever been attracted to a total stranger and didn't know what to do about it? And then, what did you do about it?

Hmm? Sounds like it might be a trick question, but yes I have. I saw this complete stranger one time in a hotel lobby. I knew he was a complete stranger because I remember thinking to myself almost immediately that that beautiful guy over there looks awfully unfamiliar. I'll bet that I haven't seen him since . . . since . . . since never.

I decided to view him from afar for awhile because I really wasn't sure what to do about him. Then, I turned my attention to my appearance. I thought to myself, "I wonder what I look like through the eyes of others? I wonder if my makeup looks okay? Is my nose longer than everyone's here or is it my imagination? Is my inside toe nail broken? My God, it is broken! And there's a horrible run in my nylons! I'm a complete mess. What will he think of me? He? Where did he go?" When I looked up he was gone.

So in answer to the question, I guess I didn't do anything about it.

We asked Littermate Brenda Barker:

How would you explain to a date that you didn't want to sleep with him?

I'd tell him that I didn't want to sleep with him. I'd say, "Lookit, I'll tickle your back, have sex with you; I'll lie down with you, shut my eyes and pretend to sleep, but I'd really prefer not sleeping with you. I just don't think I'm ready for that kind of commitment. It's too much like playing for keeps in my mind." That's what I'd say.

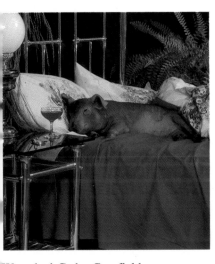

We asked Cathy Cornfield:

How would you turn a male down without hurting his feelings?

I would try to be nice. I wouldn't say no with no explanation; that's rude. So I would tell him that he is unattractive. If he said, "I am not," I'd say, "Sure you are. I'll phone my girlfriend and we'll ask her." Then I'd phone my girlfriend and say, "Is this guy over here a goon?" Then I'd hand him the phone and she'd say, "You're a goon!" 'cause we agree on everything.

If he couldn't accept that as a *no*, then I'd have to resort to nasty tactics.

SEX
WITHOUT
COLLEGE

HARD TO BELIEVE? WELL IT'S TRUE!

How many times have you been with the right person at the right time in the right place and then bingo, like a curse, you're stumped. That's right. Overcome by ignorance at that crucial moment!

It might happen something like this: "Honey, I'm going to unzip my...And then I'll...And then I'll..." And then she laughs like a witch.

Embarassing situations like this need never occur again. No more standing there drooling on your sneakers wondering how a real lover would finish the job. No more severe cases of the shrinkies through lack of know-how. We know you're probably asking yourself, as thousands of others have in the past, "But how am I going to do it without that stupid little piece of paper, that dumb certificate, without four years of college?" Stop right there! You don't have to go to college! You can learn everything there is to know right at home, in the comfort of your own garage in two weeks or less, with our SEX-BY-STEP method of teaching. You'll master everything it takes, from the very simple, "Recognizing Yourself When Naked", through to the extremely difficult, "Identifying Members of the Opposite Sex."

Accept our first installment "Why Sex At All?", FREE OF CHARGE – our gift to you, for ten days FREE inspection. Should you decide to keep it, and we're sure that you will (because it's extremely hard to return), you'll pay only $14.95 for it, and $14.95 for each of the following four installments.

Send for your FREE installment Book I today!

Clip coupon and mail to: **SEX WITHOUT COLLEGE**
2947 E. 46th St.,
N.Y.C., N.Y., 10002

YES! I want Sex Without College right away

NAME _____

ADDRESS _____

CITY _____ COUNTRY _____

LETTERS

Dear Playboar,

Taffy Lovely can eat corn chips in my bed any time! Where on earth did you rustle her up?

I was wondering if you could slip me her phone number and address? Like, I'm not a weirdo or nothing, I just want to phone her up and get to know her. She looks very friendly in the centrefold. Nobody looks like Taffy around here – except maybe the hygienist at my dentist's office. I only get to see her every six months though. Her husband works at the body shop. Judging by the job he did on my car, I doubt that I would enjoy him working on my face. So, are you going to give me her phone number and address or do I have to keep pestering you? Is she dumb or what? Everyone at work says she probably is.

– *A.L. from Iowa*

DEAR A.L.,
We're sorry, but we cannot give out phone numbers or addresses. They are confidential. We scour the world looking for the most intelligent and beautiful pigs for our centre spreads, and the Littermate of the Year is always extra special. They are not dumb! One question, if you don't mind. How did you manage to go out and buy this book, read it, and write a letter to the editor fast enough to make it into the same book? What kind of a deviant are you, anyway?

Hi! It's A.L. again.

I've just been tinkering around the kitchen in my blue bath robe. I can't sleep. Neighbors downstairs are having a bash. They've got the music turned way up. Maybe I'll put my ugly face on and go pay 'em an unexpected visit later on.

Did I ask you if you would send me Taffy Lovely's phone number and address? I haven't received anything from you yet. I keep checking the mailbox — but nothing! In answer to your question, I do remember buying the book, and I do recall writing the letter. But I don't know whether I wrote the letter before or after I bought the book. It would be safe to say that I have been drinking heavily for weeks.

– *A.L.*

Dear Playboar,

Please give this poem to Taffy Lovely. She's great!

    Bellies nipples ears and tails
    Dewy nose painted nails
    Dreamy eyes and lips like swine
    Taffy Lovely please be mine.

D.S.

DEAR D.S.,
We gave it to her! She really liked it!

Dear Playboar,

Wow! Uniformity! Check out the set of lungs on Taffy Lovely! You guys are something else. Is she for real? Now I know why I keep buying Playboar. – *S.M.*

DEAR S.M.,
We'll have to admit that Taffy's set of lungs certainly are cause for a lot of heavy breathing these days. Glad you like her!

Hey, Playboar! Remember me?

Yeah, old A.L. from Iowa. Letter number one! Numero uno dans la section de lettres! You're damn right I've been drinking! What do you expect? I've been fantasizing about Taffy for weeks. But do you send me her address? No! Do I anxiously wait and run to the mailbox twice daily? Yes!

Lookit! I've got a Masters Degree in Psychology, – I know what my problem is! But I have myself convinced that looking at a picture is not the same as enjoying in the flesh. Please convince me that I'm wrong or cough up her phone number and address! – *A.L.B.C.N.U.*

Dear Playboar,

How dare you disgrace the Miss Sow America Pageant! There isn't a sow in this country who wouldn't do practically anything for that honor. But pose in your magazine? No decent pig would! How much did you pay Taffy anyway? I hope you're satisfied! – *Initials withheld*

Dear Playboar,

My wife posed for your magazine some months ago. I haven't actually seen her since. Now, mind you, she always had her own career and has in the past been very busy. But not this busy! Her name was Melissa Muckdonald. Hopefully it still is. If you happen to know of her whereabouts, perhaps you could send me her address and phone number or have her call me at home.

– *Dick Muckdonald*

Dear Playboar,

How would one get to Butte, Montana, from here? I'm at this general store/gas bar place. They have a pay phone, but it's out of order and it doesn't look like anyone has been around here in years. Hold it! . . . No . . . Wait a second! . . . Yes, I think it is . . . Yes, here comes a car! Forget it, but thanks anyway.

Dear Playboar,

Yeah . . . Ah . . . My wife posed for your book that I just read. Her name is Taffy Lovely and I haven't seen her since. I just checked my bedroom and she isn't there. Then I peeked in the mailbox and she wasn't in there. Her career is busy but not this busy! I was wondering if you could send me her address and phone number or something? I'll be lurking forward to hearing from you. Thanks.

– *Box 177, Des Moines, Iowa.*

DEAR BOX 177,
Or may we call you Box? Congratulations on a very clever attempt. But it wasn't quite clever enough, A.L.

Dear Playboar:

Why does Mr. Psychology Degree think that Taffy Lovely would want anything to do with him even if he did have her phone number and address? I've sort of got designs on her myself. I've seen her pictures. I've read her comments. I would be far better suited to her than Professor Listening to the Beat of a Different Drum. – *M.E.*

Oh yeah? Well how'd you like to suck hoof, goofball! Let's clear these letters out of the way and see who's pig enough for Taffy! – A.L.

"Hmm… What's It say here? Useful for the short-term relief of manifestations of excessive anxiety in patients with anxiety neurosis… Well, that definitely sounds like me!"

Kirk: *More power Scotty! We're being sucked into a black hole.*

Scotty: *It's derna no use Captain! The engines just won't take it. I darsent give them any more power or they'll explode!*

Kirk: *Listen McTavish, I want more power or I'll send Spock down there to give you the Vulcan death grip.*

Scotty: *That would derna do any good Captain.*

TO BOLDLY GO WHERE NO

Spock: Scotty's right Captain, that would erna do none of us any ood. I think the logical pproach would be . . .

Kirk: Oh, shut up Spock! Mr. Sulu, how long will it take us to get to page 24 if we push the hyper-space button?

Sulu: There's a naked pig on page 24, Sir.

Kirk: What? I see. Well ask it how 2000 American greenbacks sound for the bottom corner of the page.

Spock: Captain, you forget that pigs haven't used money in over 300 years, since they conquered earth.

Kirk: What about plastic?

Spock: And pay the interest?

Sulu: There's a sixteenth of a page available on page 56.

Kirk: Hmm? That would require a considerable reduction in size . . . Double page colour spread down to a sixteenth of a page.

Sulu: Black-and-white only on that page too, Sir.

Kirk: Sulu, I don't mind being 3 centimeters tall, but I refuse to be in black and white!

Sulu: I'm afraid we derna have a choice, Captain.

Kirk: Okay Mr. Sulu, set a course for page 56.

PIGS HAVE GONE BEFORE

Perfume is a very sensual and personal thing to me... And going out on a date without cologne is like going out not completely dressed — a nice idea, but you can get arrested for it.

There is no reason in this day and age to go around smelling like a bunch of cows! For me, when

I smell good, I feel good, and when I feel good, I look great, and when I look great, how you say, the hogs... they go wild. Hamel NO. 5 is my personal scent.

Kathryn Dunhoof

GIVE HER THE SCENT THAT LINGERS

69 QUESTIONS

Sixty-nine questions was developed by Playboar so that you would know what it is that you like to do in the bedroom, what you think about sex and many other things that (A) ARE or (B) ARE NOT considered to be suitable dinner conversation. In short, it is the intention of this survey to take the nation's sexual pulse. (At the end of this survey you will be required to answer a number of questions about bowling. In preparation for these questions we ask that you bowl five games. Be sure to keep your score sheets and remember to return your shoes to the rental counter. Good luck).

1 How often do you have sex?
A. Once a day
B. Twice a day
C. Three times a day
D. A dozen or more times a day
E. You're a damn liar!

2 How would you describe your present sex life?
A. Satisfying
B. Unsatisfying
C. Non-existent
D. Gross. If you've never watched pigs in action use your imagination.

3 How does it compare with your sex life of say, ten years ago?
A. Better
B. Worse
C. None then. None now.

4 Do you think you're a good lover?
A. Yes
B. No
C. I've never worn a rubber!

5 With whom do you prefer to have sex?
A. Your spouse
B. Your lover
C. A stranger
D. Henry Kissinger
E. Jane Fonda's book of exercise
G. A side order of gravy

6 Are you intimidated when
A. Your partner wants to be on top
B. Your partner would rather watch T.V. than have anything to do with you sexually
C. Your partner runs out of the bedroom yelling, "Demon seed! Demon seed!"
D. Your girlfriend does a double take on the huge mortadellos down at the deli

7 During an evening of love making, how often would you have intercourse?
A. Once

B. Twice
C. More than ten times
D. You're a damn liar

8 How long must foreplay last before you really become aroused?
A. One second
B. Five minutes
C. Five to ten minutes
D. A week
E. More than 42 months which has really become a problem with me. It seems like every time I'm starting to get aroused it's time for the olympics again. There I'll sit in front of the T.V. concentrating only on sports, having forgotten all about her.
F. All of the above

9 What are your favourite positions for intercourse?
A. Me on top
B. Side by side
C. The pretzel position
D. Other

69
Q U E S T I O N S

10 **How often do you receive oral sex?**
A. I get it every month
B. I subscribe to it
C. I get it at the office and bring it home from time to time
D. I've seen it on the news rack, but I've never actually gotten it
E. I received it free for awhile and then I had to pay for it
F. I don't receive it, nor do I want to

11 **How do you feel about giving oral sex?**
A. I think a gift subscription is a great idea. I've given it many times on those special occasions. (birthdays, anniversaries, etc.)

12 **Who do you think in general has had more sex partners?**
A. Males
B. Females
C. Homosexuals
D. Hint: Homosexuals

13 **From what activity do you get the most intense orgasm?**
A. Golf
B. Squash
C. Yard work
D. Trivial Pursuit
E. Intercourse

14 **Do you masturbate?**
A. None of your business!

15 **If so, how often?**
A. I said, it's none of your business!

16 **Do you feel guilty about masturbating?**
A. Go away!

B. Just answer the question!
C. Why?
D. Because it's a questionnaire.
E. So!
F. You were doing fine up until now—what happened?
G. It's the subject.
H. Masturbation?
I. Yes.
J. Yes, you feel guilty or yes masturbation?
K. Stop badgering me or I'll call the police!

17 **How did you first learn about sex?**
A. My first real business deal
B. In the same sitting that I found out there's no Santa Claus. I had no problems dealing with the Santa Claus part, but I've never fully recovered from the realisation that I didn't come from the store.

18 **When did you first have intercourse?**
A. Right after I found out that I didn't come from the store.

19 **How many sexual partners have you had?**
A. None
B. 1-10
C. 10-20
D. 20-50
E. More than a 100
F. You ought to talk to a shrink about your fantasies!

20 **If there are times when you climax a little too quickly what do you do?**
A. Go for a walk, feed the ducks, and stare into the dark, murky water.
B. Laugh nervously and say, "Well, looks like the six o'clock flight arrived a little early this evening."

C. Popped in to see you—will try again later!

21 **Have you ever pretended to have an orgasm?**
A. Yes
B. No
C. Perhaps
D. Once on a business flight from Dallas to New York. The lady in the aisle seat was not amused by my pelvic gyrations, nor by my dirty talk. She demanded an adjustment on her ticket.

22 **Do you think that a large penis makes a male a more effective lover?**
A. Yes
B. No
C. I knew that they would eventually mention penis size!
D. No, because small ones are a lot better (or as the old song goes, it ain't me, it's the motion).

23 **About whom or what do you have fantasies?**
A. Movie stars
B. Sports figures
C. Co-workers
D. Lassie

24 **Have you ever had venereal disease?**
A. Yes
B. No
C. Alright! alright! Knock it off with the personal questions already!

25 **If you have had venereal disease, did you inform the person or persons who infected you or the person or persons you may or may**

not have infected?

A. Yes, I phoned but when they said hello I got clammy, so I pretended I was an insurance salesman.

B. Did you make any sales?

C. Two for sures, and one maybe.

26 **Is breast size important to a female's sexiness?**

A. Yes

B. No

C. Perhaps, but I can't remember.

D. Yabbut yours are still nice!

E. Don't be ridiculous, of course I still find you attractive!

F. That's not a fair question to ask anyone!

G. Because if I say yes, you'll go on a bummer!

H. Small is beautiful!

I. What do you mean, 'Is bigger more beautiful?'

J. Well, big is nice too.

K. Leave Jennifer out of it!

L. Because, she's history, that's why!

M. Okay, so I've talked to her twice in the last month!

N. Alright, three times!

O. Hers were a nice size.

P. I don't know!

Q. Because I don't carry a tape measure around with me, that's why!

R. Let's just drop the subject.

S. Because, I think you're trying to railroad me into an argument! I'll take the train back home feeling crummy, you'll phone at 3:00 a.m. and want me to apologize for something that I didn't want to say in the first place!

T. That's exactly the way it will end up!

U. Because it's happened a hundred times before!

V. I just don't understand it! You're a dynamo in your job, you knock them out at seminars but when it comes down to dealing with small tits you get all weird!

W. What, pray tell, is "aha" supposed to signify?

X. I meant dealing with the idea of small . . .

Y. I won't go ahead and say it!

Z. Don't ask me to say stupid things!

AA CUP. Okay. Jennifer's were much bigger. I like bigger because bigger is better. Big is beautiful, small is not. I love Jennifer, and that's why you're here and she isn't. Television dials would describe yours—melons would describe Jennifer's. Now, tell me honey, is that what you wanted to hear?

27 **Which of the following mollusks would you consider sleeping with?**

A. Octopus

B. Cuttlefish

C. Oyster

D. Mussel

E. Limpet

F. Snail

G. Other (specify)

28 **How do you let your partner know that you're interested in sex?**

A. By flirting and talking suggestively

B. My partner can tell

C. By kissing her passionately and not letting up until it's all over

D. Sharades

E. I lie on my back like the dog when he wants his tummy rubbed.

F. I spell "time for sex" on little sheets of bristol board using tiny bits of uncooked macaroni. When the glue dries I distribute my creations to every room in the house.

G. First of all I shot two moose last fall. I arranged to have one of the heads made into a wall trophy. The

taxidermist removed the antlers from the other one and added a leather harness so that they can be strapped on my head. When I want sex, I put them on and do a head bunting ritual with the trophy. My wife usually steps in after I've knocked the poor beast silly and leads me off to the bedroom. The little bugger's tough though. One time he went 15 rounds with me. It drove my wife mad with desire—she didn't even let me get the antlers off.

29 **If you're dissatisfied with your present relationship, what's stopping you from leaving this instant?**

A. I'll never find anyone else

B. I promised God in front of witnesses. Then of course, there were the showers and stags. The guilt from the bloody gifts alone would probably make me do something drastic (i.e. take hostages). I could not handle the "gimme back the pop-up toaster" nightmare, or the waking up in a "We're coming to pick up the macramé wall-hanging" cold sweat. I quite simply couldn't cope.

C. I play ringette with her father every Wednesday night.

D. I'm weak! I've always been weak! I'll never be any different! I could leave, alright, but where the devil am I going to go? Take the bus to Fresno? While she's back here with him? Not on your life, Bozo! The only criticism I have of my wife is that she's insensitive to my needs, knows my weak spots and plays on them heavily, comes in at three o'clock in the morning and insists that she only popped out to the Dairy Queen for a cone, constantly talks of her sexual escapades as a single sow and . . . and . . . and come to think of it, Fresno might be nice this time of year.

E. Other (specify)

30 **What's the best moment in intercourse?**
A. Foreplay
B. When my partner has the "Big O"
C. When I have the "Big O"
D. When it's over
E. Speaking in tongues
F. Chinese food afterwards

31 **Do you ever engage in any of the following?**
A. S & M
B. C & W (my last trip to Nashville was one of the highlights of my life)
C. AM
D. FM

32 **Where are some of your favorite places for intercourse?**
A. The lawn furniture
B. The washroom on the train
C. In restaurants, right after the waiter says "Anything for dessert this evening?"
D. The bedroom
E. Other (specify)

33 **How do you find sex?**
A. I find it delightful
B. I don't look forward to it
C. I find it, alright!
D. Sex finds me!

34 **How would you change your sex life to make it better?**
A. I'd have sex
B. I'd have more sex
C. I'd act out fantasies more often
D. During sex, I'd drone like they do in some of those Eastern religions

35 **How often do you have intercourse without having sex?**
A. Only once a week
B. Twice a year
C. This is a trick question—you're

on T.V. right now—is there anyone at home that you'd like to say hello to?

36 **What do you do about contraception the first time you have sex with someone?**
A. Nothing, because she can't get pregnant the first time
B. I tell them not to worry because the dentist sterilized me taking an X-ray once
C. Do they believe you?
D. Sometimes

37 **What birth-control method do you use?**
A. Condom
B. Pill
C. I fall asleep before we get to the sex part
D. I.U.D.
E. Diaphragm
F. Foam or jelly
G. Jam or chutney
H. Soup or juice?
I. Does a chef's salad come included with that?
J. No. It's extra.
K. Forget it then.
L. Mashed or fries?
M. Mashed . . . No wait! . . . Give me the fries . . . No, forget it! I'll stick with the mashed!
N. I'm sorry sir, we're on computer here. The order has already gone in and you'll have to stick with the fries.
O. That's ridiculous!
P. Maybe so
Q. Rhythm method

38 **How would you tell your partner to give you more pleasure during sex?**
A. Praise the things that she does that I like the best
B. Large charts with lots of easy to understand graphs and illustrations
C. Everything will be nice if you'd just put your hand here, honey

39 **Have you ever had fantasies about being sexually humiliated?**
A. Fantasies? I'm humiliated every time I have sex!

40 **How comfortable are you talking about sex?**
A. I'm not at all comfortable! Get off my property! Sick 'em Friskie!

41 **If you are a male are there times when you feel that you climax too quickly?**
A. How quick is too quick, and name the civil servant we're paying to measure this sort of activity?!

42 **If you have had an extramarital affair what did it offer you that your marriage didn't?**
A. An affair

43 **Have you ever suspected your partner of having an affair while you were in a relationship?**
A. No, but I'm suspicious that she may have had an affair while I was in the basement once.

69 **What is the single most sensitive part of your body?**
A. Head
B. Thorax
C. Abdomen
D. Antennae
E. Genitals

*Originally there were 69 questions. However, we felt that twenty-five of them were too unhealthy for anyone to ponder. Some of you will know which questions they were.

? ? ?

Answer **YES** or **NO** to the following:
___ Are you a loser at love, but a winner at bowling?
___ Are you a loser at bowling?
___ Are you just a loser?
___ Are you a league bowler?
___ Since this survey are you thinking of becoming a league bowler?

Dial-A-Pig

THE ULTIMATE IN TELEPHONE SEX

At Dial-A-Pig the customer comes first. We guarantee it!
Call this toll free number **1-800-769-PIGS**. If busy call **1-800-769-OINK**.
Our piglets are standing by.

Hello?

You grunt and snort in your sleep!

Yes, and you hog the blankets. What time did you leave this morning?

5:30. You looked exhausted lying there. I guess I really did a number on you.

I miss you already!

You're missing something else – aside from a few screws. Have you looked in the bathroom yet?

Why?

I took your bottle of Porko Rubanno cologne.

You thievin' little piglet. What on earth for?

I'm going to smear it all over me when I get into bed tonight … and then I'll remember everything about you … and last night!

Do you know what this call is doing to me?

I have an imagination too, you know. My plane is leaving … see you next Friday. Can I bring you anything?

My Porko Rubanno, and don't forget!

Porko Rubanno
A male's cologne
What is remembered is what isn't forgotten

Playboar is proud to introduce the winners of THE CURL NEXT DOOR photo contest. One of these beauties could be living right next door to you, but you would never in your wildest dreams have suspected her of this brand of exhibitionism. (You were mowing the lawn, the Hendersons were snapping pictures).

We aren't sure why anyone would send naked photos of themselves in to magazines, but they do. We were overwhelmed. We never once encouraged this sort of thing – it just happened. So, what were we to do? True, we could have blackmailed the senders of this off-colour material, but that would have been difficult. So, we gave in and decided to do the next best thing: hold a contest. After all, you went to the expense of accumulating the necessary equipment, not to mention shipping the kids off to camp for a week.

Glancing over these pages some of you will, no doubt, be disappointed to notice that you are not here. Sorry ladies, but we took the liberty of separating the beauties from the beasts. It was not an easy task.
Congratulations and a toast to the winners! Here you are in living colour.
The best of the Curls Next Door!

"WHO IS THAT PIG BEHIND THOSE FOSTER GRUNTS?"

 There she is,
bacon in the sun.
She caught me staring at her
in the airport in L.A.
What is she doing
here in the Virgin Islands?
She doesn't strike me as the type.
Hmm...A little swine,
a little wine,
a little romance...
Maybe I'll stroll over there
and find out.
My glasses!
Where are my glasses?

Foster Grunts... Because good times don't <u>just</u>* happen.

"And…It's good!"

TAFFY LOVELY

From Miss Sow America to Playboar's Littermate of the year

"I am an exceptionally private sow. I must admit, I had some strange feelings when I was first asked to appear in Playboar. I had to think long and hard before I agreed to appear nude in this book. Then, BING! I thought, what the hell! It's all a matter of context. If my body is treated as a thing of beauty and not just a plaything, then I'm proud and happy to let everyone view it with pleasure. The money had *nothing* to do with it."

"The pig in my life need not be conventionally handsome. Perfect snout and heavy-boned

gets boring after a while. I want a guy with unusually interesting looks."

"Winning the Miss Sow America Pageant was the second biggest thrill of my life. It takes a lot of talent and hard work to win something like that. Unfortunately, once you've won, it's not the sort of thing that if you kept the receipt you can return it if it doesn't suit. I found a better method of returning the crown. And here I am!"

"I just couldn't see myself travelling around for a whole year smiling and waving, then

"I love the sea, the feel of salt water lapping my body. I believe that the ocean currents determine the rhythm of my life."

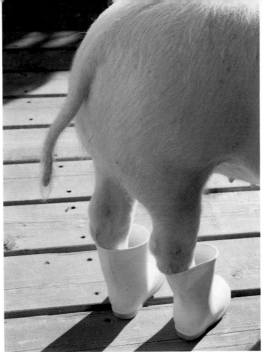

*Hunka hunka
burnin' love*

marrying a quarterback, working as a consultant selling cosmetics in a major department store and getting fat. The idea didn't excite me. I plan to marry a film producer. Then and only then will I concentrate on getting fat."

"Although they stripped me of my crown, I still got to be Miss Sow America. They can't take that away from me. I won for my talents, and now I'm even more talented. The Playboar deal brought me fame, fortune, movie offers and a chance to get on the talk show circuit."

*"I like my boars hot
and my beer cold."*

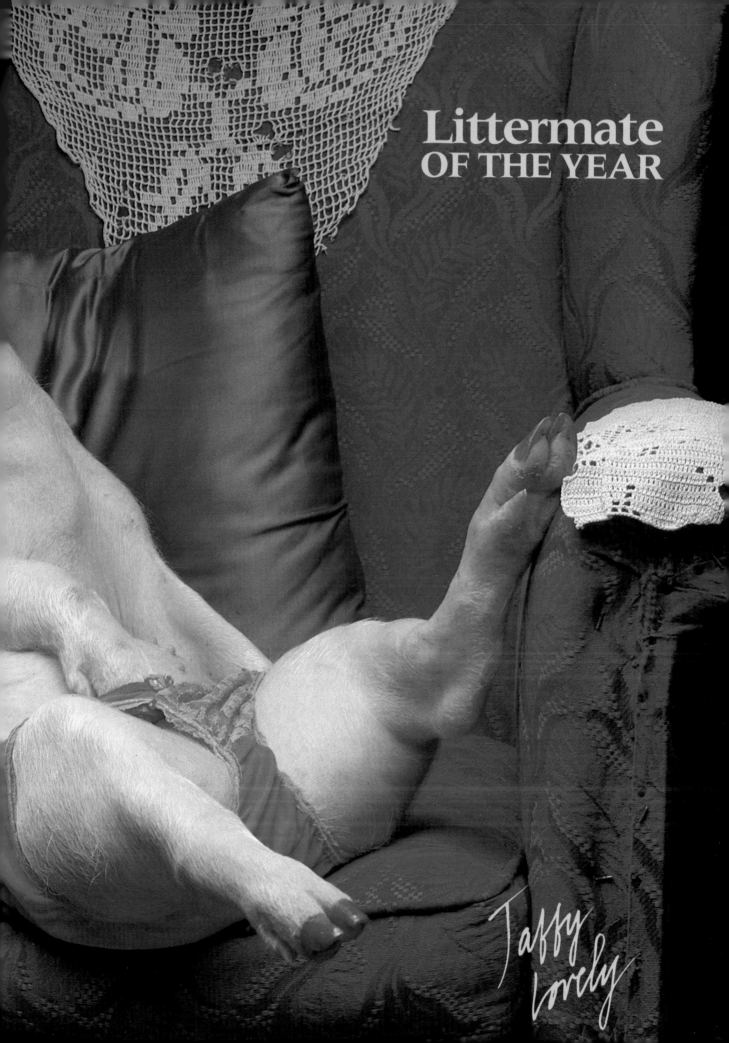

Littermate
OF THE YEAR

Taffy Lovely

Littermate Data Sheet

Name: *Taffy Lovely*

Measurements: *24-26-22*   Height: *1'4"*   Weight: *65 lbs.*

Age: *8 weeks*

Astrological Sign: *Sowjatarius*

Favourite Color: *Red*

Turn Ons: *Driving fast, big dogs, aggressive males who know who they are without having to look at their driver's licence.*

Turn Offs: *Driving slow, chi hua huas, clueless males who don't know if they're punched or boared.*

Fantasy: *Like every sow, I wanted to be Miss Sow America and Playboar's Littermate of the Year all at the same time. I don't have any more fantasies that I want to tell you about. So there!*

Ambitions: *Get into movies, make a lot of money, and retire by the age of two.*

Favourite Movies: *Rooters of the Lost Ark, The French Lieutenant's Sow, Indihama Jones (In The Temple of Fumes), Bored n' Airy People.*

Travel Plans: *I want to visit Club Mud to meet strangers with problems.*

Overcome by an irresistable urge, Melvin, the janitor,
sprang the ultimate practical joke.

HOMO FILE

Rent A

Fresh
Pork S

Save .80 lb.

CENTRAL · INTELLIGRUNTS · AGENCY ·

PIGUS
SNEAKAROUNDICUS

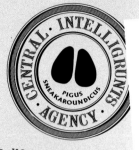

As a result of much investigation worldwide it is necessary to make the following statement:

It is the opinion of this agent that HOMO SAPIENS cannot be trusted. In a multitude of ways they pose a rather large threat to the security of all pigs everywhere. THEY ARE DANGEROUS!!!

Pigs were targets in NATO exercise

By IAN MATHER
Observer News Service

BARDU, Norway—When more than 25,000 troops took part in a mock invasion of northern Norway last week there were six fatalities, all of them pigs. The animals were used by military surgeons to practice treating bullet wounds in field hospitals.

Each pig was anesthetized before being suspended by its legs from a wooden frame and then shot.

A Norwegian soldier crouched in the snow 10 metres from one pig and shot it through the right leg with a high-velocity rifle. Then he took out a pistol and shot it at close range through the abdomen.

A team of medical orderlies bandaged the pig's leg, wrapped it in a blanket, placed it on a stretcher and rushed it to a field hospital in a military ambulance.

There, in a tent set up as an operating room, military surgeon Captain Reidar Eikehaugen of Spitzbergen and his team performed a two-hour operation. When the operation was completed the pig was killed and its body burned.

"On the battlefield we might have to destroy bodies, so we are practicing how to do that,"

said Colonel Jens Nygard, head of veterinary services for the Norwegian Armed Forces. "The use of pigs is the only realistic way to train surgeons in the treatment of bullet wounds."

Col. Nygard said the pig was shot twice to give the surgeons training on wounds from both high-velocity bullets, which cause extreme shock to the surrounding muscles, and from slower-moving pistol bullets.

"Sometimes the pig is not shot correctly, and the wounds are so severe that the pig dies on the operating table," he added. "But that also is realistic because it happens in war."

Last week's military exercise was designed to test the ability of the North Atlantic Treaty Organization to reinforce the far north of Norway, which is immediately contiguous to the Soviet Union, in winter conditions.

A flotilla of 130 warships from NATO countries landed a large force that was supposed to be Russian, in fjords south of Tromso above the Arctic Circle. Western troops rushed to the area to try to drive back the invaders.

The exercise was reported to Warsaw Pact countries in advance...

Arafat Linked With Cows

MIDDLE EAST (N.F.A.) — Yassar Arafat has been under suspicion for harboring cows. A source has revealed that Arafat supports the cows in their terrorist activities.

In solidarity with that other great benefactor of brute terrorism, Moomar Gaddaffy, Arafat stated, "I will always come to the aid of my good friends the cows." Cows have claimed responsibility for carrying out a string of *barnyard style* bombings and killings worldwide. It is believed that Arafat and the P.L.O. have been supplying arms and offering refuge to terrorist cows for some 18 months now.

RENTER	Colonel Jens Nygard
ADDRESS	Fort Bardu, Tent # 42
CITY Bardu	**COUNTRY** Norway
AGE 57	**OCCUPATION** Veterinarian (of sorts)
EMPLOYER Norwegian Armed Forces	

Rent A PIG®

"NORWAY'S LARGEST RENTER OF PIGS"

RENTAL AGREEMENT
Terms and Conditions

Rentor hereby rents to the renter, the pig, subject to the terms and conditions contained below.

1. **ABUSE OF THE PIG:** Renter acknowledges receiving the pig in good condition. Renter undertakes that he will drive and operate the pig at all times with care and prudence. Renter is responsible for all damage to the pig, attributable, in the Rentor's sole opinion, to abusive operation and undertakes to pay the Rentor the cost of repairing all abuse damage to the satisfaction of the Rentor. Abusive operation shall include but not be limited to:
a) Operation of the pig on unpaved highways, roads, streets, or in military field hospitals.
b) Failure to check or maintain fluid levels (ie. blood) in pig during operation.
2. **SEVERE BODILY DAMAGE:** The Rentor will not be liable if the pig(s) pull a mental and cause severe bodily damage to others when:
Scenario 1
The pigs are pinned down in a bunker about a half-mile inside enemy lines. They've been under heavy enemy fire for a number of hours. They realize that their only option is to break loose and cause severe bodily damage to their aggressors. Rent-A-Pig will not be held responsible.
Scenario 2
The pigs are told they are going for a nice walk, and if they're really good, perhaps a picnic later. They get about as far as Northern Norway and they are seized, hung up and told that they will be shot with high velocity bullets. If the pigs resist, break loose, and cause severe bodily damage to their aggressors, Rent-A-Pig will not be held responsible.
Scenario 3
The pigs are shown a map of Norway. On this particular map, Northern Norway has been noticeably scratched out and in its place, hastily pencilled-in, appear the words 'Grandma's House'. The pigs are told that the Communists (The Big Bad Wolf) want to kill Grandma and roast her in the oven over at Hansel and Gretel's place. But, before arriving at H&G's there was some mention of popping in to the Three Bear's house where they would walk in just in time to hear Baby Bear deliver the line: "Somebody's been shot with high velocity rifles in

my bed and they're still here!" The pigs, suspecting that the above is an elaborate trap, break loose, go wild and cause severe bodily harm to their aggressors. Rent-A-Pig will not be held responsible.
3. **REPAIRS:** Renter shall not permit any repairs to the pig or allow any lien* to be placed on the pig or removed from the pig. The Renter shall be liable for such repairs.
*This also applies to any fat.
4. **ACCIDENTS:** Renter shall, within 24 hours of its occurence, report any accident to the law enforcement agency having jurisdiction at the place of the accident and to the Rentor.
5. **THEFT OF PIG:** The Renter is responsible for any theft of the pig, unless the keys are removed, doors locked and the windows closed tightly.
6. **RETURN OF THE PIG:** If the pig(s) are not returned by the due back time they are assumed stolen.

CONTRACT AGREEMENT

I Jens Nygard am the Renter of __6__ pig(s) and will be the sole drover of the mentioned pig(s) and to the best of my knowledge will not be exposing the pig(s) to any unrealistically bizarre military exercises and agree to return the pig(s) to Rent-A-Pig undented. I have personally inspected the pig(s) and have found them to be dent-free.
Answer 'yes' or 'no' to the following:

NO Do you plan to take the pig(s) out of the country?

NO Will the pig(s) take part in a mock invasion of Northern Norway?

NO Will the pig(s) be shot with high velocity rifles and then barbecued?

SIGNED X	Jens Nygard
WITNESS X	Rent A Pig

INVOICE NUMBER 15227

NAME

MEET ANGEL

NOW ONLY $59.⁹⁵ COMPLETE

YOUR NEW COMPANION

Wouldn't it be nice to have a companion of your very own – someone you could love and who would always love and respect you? Sure it would! And here's the best part: She's never too tired, she never ever says no, and she has never been fussy about looks. Another comforting feature is that Angel only says "Yes" to you. Now that *is* comforting to know! And, just think, if your buddies drop around for a beer during the day, Angel's Legs-o-lock* feature makes her say, "No way José".

Think of how Angel could change your life! That's right, Angel will be there when you need her. Angel comes in a plain box, blows up in minutes, and she's made of a Durable Kind of Weird Stuff.* Nothing is too wild or too schmaltzie for Angel. Angel is the original and best blow-up doll on the market today – don't be fooled by imitations!

Her lips seem to move when she talks. Cassette or 8-track squeals 10 different things:

1. "I love you *blank*" (give preferred name with order)
2. "No way José" (to your so-called buddies)
3. "Faster!"
4. "More toast honey?"
5. "I need some money to go shopping."
6. "Another beer dear?"
7. "But aren't zucchini for eating!"
8. "You don't ever have to take me on holidays."
9. "I like to be kept waiting!"
10. "You're the best I've ever had!"

*ANGEL and LEGS-O-LOCK are registered trademarks of PERV-O-PRODUCTS INC. DURABLE KIND OF WEIRD STUFF is a registered trademark of the DUPANT COMPANY.

HOW TO BE

A Swine's Guide to Etiquette

A PROPER BOOR

PREFACE

It is most difficult to master the ways of a boor. More difficult perhaps than to live one's life in a mannerly manner. It is, of course, scarcely possible that anything original should be found in a volume like this, as almost all that it contains must have fallen under the notice of every swine of penetration who has the habit of frequenting "Vulgar Society".

This volume is almost beyond criticism. It has no pretentions as a literary work, and is not intended to be judged as such, its sole merit depending upon its correctness and fitness of application.

1

TABLE MANNERS: ARE THERE SUCH THINGS?

Yes indeed there are and in a word, 'vulgar', sums them up. To make impressions at the table one need only remember the following:

Cutlery was invented by a moron. All food should simply be transported from hoof to mouth. Cutlery does however, have its use.

Spoons

Spoons should be used for boinking other guests and/or launching pits.

Forks

Forks are very useful in the stealing of food. They are also ideal for ruining the enamel on one's teeth, when one ventures to use the instrument as a tool for removing food particles which have become lodged between two or more of one's teeth.

Knives

Knives should be used first, for defending one's own dinner and second, for swiping butter from other dinner guests' knives.

There was a time when those of polite society believed that food should be passed nicely. Today, thank goodness, all that has changed. At last food is tossed and rifled as it should be.

A note to beginner boors: Buns are particularly well-designed for the practise of catapulting.

2

GRABBING AT THE WAITRESS

Why is it that waitresses encourage grabbing? I don't know either, but they do. Management will not care if you grab its staff. As we're sure you've found in most restaurants today, employees understand that being mauled is part of the service they're expected to provide. It also lightens the tone of the business lunch, usually getting at least one good guffaw. Pinching her on the buttocks is equally acceptable, although grabbing is perhaps more popular.

3

HOW MUCH SHOULD I STIFF THE WAITER?

As we've all found, the quality of service in restaurants varies from establishment to establishment and from waiter to waiter and even from night to night, given the same waiter. This can be confusing.

Naturally, if the service is very poor, you are going to stiff the waiter a lot less. However, if the service and food are exceptional, then of course you'll want to stiff the waiter a great deal more. In any event, tipping is for bimbos.

4

CONVERSING WITH SOWS

If you are desirous of pleasing a young sow, whether she is pretty or otherwise, always endeavor to appear interested in her conversation, however stupid it may be.

Sample Conversation

Sow: And, then I thought to myself, 'But what if I don't look good in the blue dress? Perhaps I'd best try the red dress on, for the third time.' So I tried it on and believe me I looked just like a street-walker. Well, I wasn't about to be going around like that. So, after I tried the blue dress on again I decided to take it.

You: Well, well, that's fascinating!

5

DATING AND FORNICATION – DO WE SLEEP TOGETHER ON THE FIRST DATE?

No *we* don't. But you and your lady friend should.

6

WHO SLEEPS ON THE WET SPOT?

It is most difficult for anyone to give in to slumber when one's hip is resting on the wet spot. Someone must sleep on it, but whom shall it be?

Traditionally, it is the female who sleeps on the wet spot. There is nothing to be gained by breaking with tradition.

7

SUBSTITUTES FOR SEX

Many sows feel that Scrabble is a nice change from sex. It is neither a nice change, nor is it a substitute. Just as meaningful conversation, cold showers, watching T.V., changing fuses, leapfrogging or hosing the lawn are not substitutes. It is safe to say, that there's no real substitute for sex.

8

APRÉS FORNIQUÉ

After a round of sex there is always that question. Who puts the Dream Whip back in the refrigerator? And while she's at it, who fetches the glass of water? Traditionally it is the female.

9

THE PATERNITY SUIT

As far as the paternity suit goes, one only need say: "I wasn't at that party! You were pregnant when I got there, and, um, we went home alone. And furthermore, I've never seen you before!"

10

HEY LADY, I CAN SEE UP YOUR DRESS

If you can in fact see up her dress, it is considered to be in extremely good taste to bring the matter to her attention.

11

MISS SIMPSON HAS RATHER LARGE BREASTS AND NO DOUBT SOMETHING SHOULD BE SAID TO HER ABOUT THEM – BUT WHAT?

Everyone knows a Miss Simpson. You'll find her almost everywhere. You'll see her shuffling papers, on the subway, at the fish market, stopping traffic, or just picking up a few items from the convenience store. Miss Simpson has two very noticeable attributes. That's right, the same ones that your eyes wander to at least a dozen times during a conversation with her. No doubt something should be said to her about them — but what? Remember, Miss Simpson will not be offended if you speak up because she loves the attention and will probably be upset if you don't.

Something to Say

1. "Miss Simpson, I must commend you on your rather large breasts!"
2. "Miss Simpson, may I commiserate with you on bearing the burden of your rather large breasts. Allow me to lend them a hoof."

12

VISITING THE PSYCHIATRIC PATIENT

Treat any psychiatric patient the same way as you would treat any other . . . psychiatric patient. With extreme caution! This isn't the Fred you knew. He's somebody else now. He's not in there for a holiday! He's there because it is the opinion of a doctor who spent eleven years in university that the patient you are about to visit is 'Nutso'.

When visiting, it is always wise to sit in the chair by the door, furthest away from Mr. Unpredictable, even if it means using a megaphone to converse.

If the patient reaches for the top drawer of the night table to offer you a chocolate, as they so often do, be prepared to bolt for the parking lot. Remember, chocolates are kept in the second drawer, scissors are stored in the top.

Tell him that it's okay to cry. Suggest to him that someone who cares should be looking after his money matters. Someone like yourself. Reassure him that he will be helping himself by signing 'Fred' beside the x's. Then scurry out to the nurses' station before he changes his minds.

13

BLACKMAIL

The Concept

A picture is worth a thousand words/bucks. Many pictures are worth many thousands of words/bucks. Many, many explicit pictures taken by someone who obviously knew what they were doing, are worth whatever the market will bear, and considerably more if the blackmailee happens to be in politics.

The Letter

Mr. John Blank   The Date
7 Clearview Ave.
Compromised, U.S.A.

Dear John,

I sincerely hope that you had fun last weekend. Judging by some of these snapshots, it appears as though you did. Boy, you sure look funny in leotards! Both the whirlpool and clothes line shots turned out great. Of course with these new auto-focus cameras, even an idiot can take perfect pictures. I took the film to one of those "in by nine out by five" photo labs — got an extra set of prints for only a dollar. How do they do it?

Anyway John, what are you doing next Saturday? Let's get together or something. How does the Eight Ball Lounge at the Bond Street Hotel sound? Say, two p.m.? Bring a thousand dollars. I'll be wearing a rabbit suit!

Forever yours,

OBJECTING AT THE WEDDING

INTERIOR/CHURCH/DAY
Wedding ceremony in progress.

MINISTER
Therefore, if anyone can show any just
cause, why they may not lawfully be
joined together, let them speak now
or forever hold their peace.

*The preacher looks up ceremoniously and is
about to continue when a boor speaks up in a
loud voice.*

BOOR
Reverend. Can I talk to you? I know
it's a bad time. But, can I talk to you?
I, as well as a good number of the male
members of this congregation have
been intimate with her! (Points to
BRIDE) *We all **know** her . . . if you
catch my drift . . .*

*Camera cuts to bride. Bride looks mortified.
Camera cuts to BRIDE'S PARENTS. Bride's parents look appalled. Cut to close up of ceiling
painting of Mary Magdalene. Camera pans
across 20 OLD BOY FRIENDS snickering in
back row. Cut TO B.C.U. (Big close-up) of
GROOM's face. Groom's eye is twitching, his
nostrils are flared and his mouth is quivering.*

BOOR (Continues)
. . . Therefore, we find this little tramp
to be a most unsuitable spouse for
Trevor . . . Forget it! It doesn't matter . . . I was just thinking out loud.

CHOKING CERTAIN INDIVIDUALS

Every self-respecting boor has a wild and crazy
streak which needs to be exercised from time
to time. It's no secret that there are certain in-
dividuals out there who lend themselves particularly well to the practice of choking. You
will know who they are when you meet them.
Remember: *They* provoked *you*. It's their own
damn fault!

PROPER USE OF THE 'F' WORD

The 'F' word has totally lost its original mean-
ing. It was a very effective word when it meant
what it used to mean, and it is most certainly
very useful now – we think. It should be used
in polite conversation as much as possible.

IF I THINK IT'S OKAY DO I DO IT?

There are so many pitfalls in the world of social
intercourse wherein it would be most improper
to do what *seems* to be okay. If you have mas-
tered proper boor etiquette, use your own vulgar
judgement. When in doubt, do the opposite of
what seems to be okay.

ENVOY

*Follow the suggestions herein imparted, and
you will become a swine of penetration.*

PLAYBOAR FUNNIES

HAM RADIO

"Every Thursday, Lincoln would lure the cows into the bus and take them for a bit of a joy ride which almost always scared the hell out of them."

HOW TO PICK UP A PIG

YOU WILL POSSESS POWER OVER PIGS!

And now from the author who brought us his best selling novelty, "How to Make Love To A Boar", comes an entirely new book that is sure to shake the world of sexual literature. **HOW TO PICK UP A PIG**, will change your life! Are you discouraged because you go out to the pick-up bars and spend $300 in an evening sending those fancy drinks with the tiny umbrellas and the attractive fruit garnish over to every pig in the place with little or no results? Well, there is no longer any reason to be feeling single and seeing double at the end of an expensive evening.

Take a cue from someone who bought and read the book and was overwhelmed by the results.

"I sat back for years, my little heart pounding like a frightened bird's, while confident boars harvested all the good looking pigs before my very eyes! I was depressed! Then I responded to an ad, similar to this one, and purchased the **HOW TO PICK UP A PIG** book. This may sound outrageous, but after reading only two chapters I went out and picked up not one, but two pigs, the very first night. It may only be a skinny paperback, but I spend hundreds less per night on booze and have pigs stampeding to get at me because now, 'I POSSESS POWER OVER PIGS'!"

Fill in coupon and include **$29.95** for each book ordered.

It's genius Doctor!

SPRIGS FOR PIGS™ Hair Replacement

Before

After

Unretouched photographs of an actual client of SPRIGS FOR PIGS™

'AND THEN ONE MORNING I AWOKE AND IT WAS ALL OVER THE SHEETS!'

'I used to think when my hair was falling out in wads, that I didn't have any choice about it. I hated wearing a hair piece and absolutely refused to have surgery.

'Frankly my hair, or lack of it, really did bother me. You know, I'm a young guy, I'm into music, I like hanging around steam baths and I just didn't feel right about growing bald. Then I found out about **SPRIGS FOR PIGS**™ hair replacement. I was really quite nervous at first and very skeptical but they were very nice and I found out about this fantastic new process called the ***Tuft-by-Tuft***® System. They actually build body back into thinning hair by adding real pigs' hair in with your own—one tuft of hair at a time. It's a unique process that requires some drilling, but no more "Hey cue ball!" and no more fishing the hair piece out of the pool filter. It looks perfectly natural.

'I still swim and jog like always but now, thank goodness, I don't have to worry about my hair. You really ought to try them.'

Naughty Dottie

Playboar let's you draw the line

"Hoggy Style"

The Pig Times

SPECIAL EDITION — YESTERDAY'S NEWS TODAY — A BUCK THREE SIXTY

PIGS MAY SUE BULL TERRIERS

BOSTON (ROOTERS)— Contract negotiations have been slow and tempers have been high during the past few weeks as Pigs battle it out with Bull Terriers for a settlement in their controversial impersonation contract dispute.

William "The Killer" Bacono, lawyer and spokespig, is demanding $7 million over five years for the I.A.P.P. (International Association of Practising Pigs) from the B.T.D. (Bull Terrier Dogs) as payment for their continued impersonation of pigs. Bacono said that if they couldn't reach an agreement soon, they might be forced into a lawsuit.

"THEY'LL PAY FOR THEIR INSTANT CREDIBILITY" SAID BACONO IN AN INTERVIEW

They'll pay for their instant credibility," said Bacono in an interview.

Lassie

PAY OR GO BACK TO LOOKING LIKE LASSIE!

Bacono has given the Terriers an ultimatum: "Pay or go back to looking like Lassie!" He went on to say that Bull Terriers are not really a breed at all.

They were in fact, radical Scotch Collies who broke away from the breed in 1962. One of the conditions of the break-away was that they stop looking like Lassies, (Scotch Collies). The radicals complied with all conditions of the break-away and in 1962 adopted a new look that would win them instant approval.

It did just that. In 1963, they entered into a twenty-year, $5 million contract which expired last year.

The new five-year, $7 million contract met with immediate rejection by angry Bull Terriers. Pigs have been without a contract for ten months while the pig dogs continue their lucrative impersonations.

FOOLING OUR SOWS

Bacono complained that Bull Terriers have been taking advantage of fringe benefits reserved only for pigs.
The new contract will contain a "paws off our sows" clause.

THEY'RE TAKING OUR JOBS

Bacono told The Pig Times that they, the pig dogs, are taking our jobs. It is estimated that 250,000 Bull Terriers now occupy job positions that would normally have been filled by pigs—"Because of their phoney likeness to pigs!" said Bacono.

WE'LL GO BANKRUPT

Slumpy Fulton, spokespig for the Terriers, said, "$7

Slumpy Fulton

million over five years is ludicrous. Fetching the stick just doesn't pay well enough to warrant that kind of spending—even with all our members contributing." Fulton added, "We either spread that $7 million over 10 years, or go bankrupt."

SMELLY AILMENT BAFFLES DOCTORS

SYDNEY (ABO)—Doctors at a major Sydney, Australia, hospital are most perplexed by an ailment that causes a 25-year old sow to give off an odor like stinky feet. A specialist in Smelly Illnesses and Stinky Diseases said he has been unable to identify the syndrome, despite a computer search of ~~medieval~~ medical literature. The sow, who lives in Sydney, feels intense warmth over her face, legs and hams, followed by an unbearable itching and the ghastly odor. The episodes began a year ago, occuring every few days at first. But now, they occur daily and last for several hours. Although she hasn't bathed in eight months and plays a lot of indoor sports, (floor hockey, basketball, squash), her body still gives off an odor like stinky feet, doctors said. Another symptom is that she hasn't been asked out in about eight months. Doctors add, "We may or may not have ruled out personal hygiene as a cause."

BIG HEADLINE
WITH NO STORY SPARKS INQUEST
HEARING TOLD – STORY TO FOLLOW UNLIKELY

Continued on page 5

SOVIET SWINE BOMBARD BRAINS WITH BEAMS

WASHINGTON 10AM— The Soviet Union has achieved "significant progress" toward developing mind-control weapons, according to a United States Army study focusing on military uses of psychic phenomenon.

"Soviet scientists view the brain as an apparatus available for probing and manipulation," said an army spokespig.

Speculation over possible motives behind the Soviet bombardment of the U.S. Embassy in Moscow focused largely on the use of beams to jam U.S. electronic intelligence-gathering equipment. However, another hypothesis is that the Soviets are using radiation to effect mind-changes.

There are a number of large U.S. corporations suspected of using, for advertising purposes, services offered by Soviet mind-bombarding agencies. Among them are: Burger King during *NATIONAL SWITCH WEEK;* Pepsi Cola for *THE PEPSI CHALLENGE;* and the Chrysler Corporation for their *SAY 'YES' TO CHRYSLER* campaign.

The thought of American companies using Soviet agencies rather than American agencies for these services distresses the U.S. Army Marketing Analysis Bureau but has the Soviets . . . well . . . positively beaming.

KREMLIN WORKER KILLED BY EXPLODING POTATO

An unidentified Kremlin worker was killed today when the potato he was ~~driving swerved to miss a microwave beam, smashed through guard rail, and plunged into thirty foot culvert~~ heating up for lunch exploded in microwave oven. Tin foil has been named as the cause of the mishap.

Soviets Deny Worker Killed by Potato

MOSCOW—The Soviet Foreign Ministry has denied accusations that a Kremlin worker was killed by an exploding baked potato. "The allegation was invented to damage relations between the two countries and is a pile of crap," said a Soviet.

The Sow Jones Drops Another Ten

The Sow Jones has laid off another ten employees. However, the Sow Jones is not the only index axing jobs, the T.S.E., C.S.E. and the L.S.E. have also been experiencing layoffs. Chester White, of the Jones, explains that unless big business picks up, there could be more layoffs ahead.

COMMUNIST PIGS DENY WAVES USED ON EMBASSY

MOSCOW 11:15AM—The Soviet Foreign Ministry has denied accusations that the U.S. Embassy in Moscow has been bombarded by microwaves. The Soviets said the allegation was invented to damage relations between the two countries and was nothing more than a "Beeg pile of Bullshitski!"

Western journalists were told that they (the U.S.) had filed a protest with the Foreign Ministry after tests confirmed that microwaves had been beamed at the building earlier this year. The Russians have denied the incident. They did admit to using microwaves daily, "But only for heating up our lunch." The U.S. Ambassador said that microwaves are not a danger to health but he is concerned about the principle.

Suspicion rose when Embassy lunches began cooking in their bags at 9:30 in the morning—by noon the bread was so hard that you couldn't get your teeth into it and most of them had to be tossed out.

U.S. SEEKS COMPENSATION IN MICROWAVE SCANDAL

The U.S. Embassy is seeking 6,000 rubles as compensation, or about 20 rubles for each of the 300 lunches destroyed in the Embassy microwave scandal. The Kremlin's reaction: "Nice try, better lunch next time!" U.S. officials are not amused.

MARKETING WORLD

MASCULINE PROTECTION PRODUCTS BOMB

The International Tissue Company is bewildered and $6 million lighter while lines of its masculine protection products are gathering dust on the shelves.

David Pumpitout, Director of Marketing for I.T.C., explains that his company was convinced that Mascupads and Lightguys would find a market of their own. "The feminist movement did not have the impact that we thought it would. Males attempting to identify with feminine problems are obviously finding other ways of doing it. New customs such as: 'Let's split the cheque' and 'Why don't you open your own damn door!' certainly bit deeply into our market share."

When asked what I.T.C. was going to do with 40 million pads that are strong enough for a sow, yet made for a boar, Pumpitout replied, "They're a nifty product and we're a smart company. I'm sure we'll find a use for them."

WEAR THEM JUST BECAUSE

And now a little something for guys, because you want to know how she feels. Because you need protection, too. Masculine protection.

"But isn't it unnatural for a guy and won't it make me howl at the moon?" you ask. Yes, it's perfectly unnatural for a guy, but no, it won't make you howl at the moon. You see, we at International Tissue developed MASCUPADS and LIGHTGUYS* because we feel that every relationship can use a little more understanding. Sure, they are somewhat of an inconvenience, but think of the advantages: "Lookit! I'm sorry! I'm edgy! I'm on the bun...Okay?" They'll understand.

Or wear them just because, because 'because' is good enough.

* MASCUPADS and LIGHTGUYS are treadmarks of International Tissue Company.

YORKSHIRE RIPPER APPEALS SENTENCE

LONDON—Peter Suttcliffe, the Yorkshire Ripper, killer of thirteen prostitutes and namesake of one of history's most notorious murderers said today, "I've had quite enough jail, thank you!"

Suttcliffe, sentenced three years ago to 13 consecutive sentences of 25 years, said that he'd never actually sat down and multiplied it out until yesterday morning. "It's not even realistic," he said. "I won't be out of here until after I'm dead. And then, what am I going to do even when I do get out?"

Suttcliffe's lawyer Peter Suttcliffe (no relation) told Judge, Sir Leslie Boreham, at London's Old Bailey, that Suttcliffe (the ripper) seemed to be straightening around. "He hasn't killed a hooker in three years! Now, Your Honour, this would indicate to me that my client has had a change of heart. You'll have to admit that that is an extremely good record for a man who was murdering an average of 2 1/6 prostitutes a year."

Judge Boreham replied, "Mr. Suttcliffe, how would you define 1/6 of a prostitute? Hmm? Would you mind doing that for the court?"

"Well, sir, she would be one that would only take you part of the way there. Approximately 1/6 of the way there, sir."

"There? Where, Mr. Suttcliffe?"

"Well . . . 'There', sir. There, where everything is sunny skies for a brief but unforgettably wonderful and most gratifying moment in time. As you come to your senses you leap to your feet and say 'I've got to get out of here! How much do I owe you? Thanks! Goodbye!' But you wouldn't get that far with 1/6 of a prostitute, sir. She might only take off her gloves

or show you her legs from the knees down."

"And how much might one of these fractional encounters cost one?"

"Oh, about 1/6 of the normal price, sir!"

"Really! Hmm . . . interesting."

"Fascinating, isn't it sir. Now, does that answer your question?"

"Well . . . yes . . . well sort of . . . perhaps we could scratch that question from the records . . . I was just curious, that's all!"

Suttcliffe's lawyer, Suttcliffe, said that Suttcliffe was willing to plead guilty to drunken driving if Judge Boreham would drop the ripper charges.

Boreham's reply was "no".

"How about a million dollars worth of parking tickets. Let's pretend my client was here for that. He obviously can't pay them but he'd be willing to serve weekends for 50 years!"

Again Boreham rejected the offer.

"Okay then, your honour, I'll give you £45,000 for the house including the half-acre property across the road and not a penny more!"

"Are you mad? Do you think that I am ignorant of its worth? I said £60,000 for the house. I keep the property across the road. Take it or leave it."

"And the tool shed, sir?"

"What of it?"

"Is it included in the deal? I think I should like it as well."

"Oh," (pause) "I suppose."

"Sold, you old goat. Now what about my client's appeal?"

"It wasn't included in the deal and you bloody well know it, Suttcliffe."

Suttcliffe's appeal for parole after serving only three years was rejected. Judge Boreham told Suttcliffe that he must serve the remaining 322 years of his sentence. "If you still feel the same way about jail after that time, I'd be more than happy to discuss it with you then."

As he was being led out of the Oak Panelled Chamber, scene of some of Britain's most celebrated trials, Suttcliffe began yelling obscenities and continued to do so all the way out to the armoured truck which took him away.

Denver Pig Charged With Carless Driving

DENVER (AP)—A Denver pig was charged Tuesday afternoon with carless driving. The case, the first of its kind in Colorado, has been gaining a lot of press over the past week.

The defendant pleaded not guilty to the charge, on the grounds that he was walking to the store for cigarettes, rather than wasting fuel by driving. Police said that the car he wasn't driving was weaving all over the road. "We simply had to pull him over," an officer said. A Denver judge told the defendant that he found his walking-to-the-store story to be the "most outrageous lie" he'd ever heard. Moments later a twelve-pig jury handed down the unanimous guilty verdict.

Shown above is the car that the Denver pig wasn't driving at the time of his arrest.

TELEPHONE SEX
Paying Through the Nose To Get It in the Ear

Say "hello" to an industry growing at such a staggering rate that it has politicians (who are not already using the service themselves) very concerned.

Telephone sex has reached such epidemic levels that the government is urging citizens not to answer their phones. Not even in an emergency. An employee of the government's newly formed Telephone Sex Emergency Task Force says there are so many of those "sexy numbers" in service, that some pigs are even afraid to call out for fear of getting a raw number.

DON'T CALL US WE'LL CALL YOU

Five hundred thousand pigs have been evacuated from a region hit hard by telephone sex. It's already been declared a disaster area.

One evacuee recalls this terrifying story: "I was watching T.V. when the phone rang. It was my neighbor. She wanted to borrow a cup of chop. There was nothing peculiar about that. She always wanted to borrow something. Then she asked me for my credit card number. I thought that was a bit strange, but I gave it to her. She said she'd slip into something a little more comfortable and call me right back. She did. Then all hell broke loose."

Petrified, he made his way down to the basement where he remained until Army helicopters arrived.

BOSLEY WARNS PIGS

Congresswine Bosley warned pigs last night. Speaking from a television studio in Climax, New York, Bosley said, "I just want to let you know that cattle have been dying in the area. Now for the bad news. We aren't sure yet how or why they are dying. For your own safety, should the telephone ring, do not answer it. Proceed single file to the basement and remain there until it has stopped ringing. And for heaven's sake, STAY AWAY FROM COWS!"

Bosley further warned pigs of tricky telephone sex solicitors who will phone, hang up as if they've given up, and then phone back immediately before residents have a chance to rush back to their basements. "Making us the sixth largest state in the union and contributing about 10% to the Gross National Product." Bosley also promised, "I will strongly urge the declaration of a national emergency to aid victims and the families of these victims."

GIMME THAT LONG DISTANCE FEELING

In almost every major city worldwide, thousands of female solicitors with little or no telephone experience give their clients "the next best thing to being there". Among those who pay through the nose for this service are perverts, misfits, the lonely, the unattractive and the unsuspecting.

THEY'LL PAY UP TO A HUNDRED DOLLARS A CRACK

The owner of a New York telephone sex company says that clients will pay between twenty and one hundred dollars a crack, so to speak.

"Although $20 to $40 is more common, wealthy clients with discriminating tastes are willing to pay extra for looks. To some, it's very important that they continue the relationship with the same pig, while the more promiscuous types want a different pig every time," he said.

TELEPHONE SEX NOT SEX WITHOUT COMMITMENT

Pigs who have given up on the more complicated, only occasionally stimulating, far-less personal-freedom, straightjacket style of relationship, i favor of the long distance lus affair are mistaken to believe there is no commitment According to a study, they sti have a big commitment to th telephone and credit car companies. "They," says th study, "can be dirtier tha any heart-broken lover."

HOW DO I DO IT?

Anyone interested in tryin telephone sex should note th following steps:
1) Dial the telephone se company of your choice.
2) Give them you neighbour's credit card number.
3) They'll check him out.
4) If he's not over his limit they'll call you back.
5) Someone talks dirty to you
6) The bill is sent to him.
7) His wife intercepts the bill
8) They have a huge argument.
9) His wife leaves him.

NEW LIGHT SHED ON GRAVE OF UNKNOWN PIG

The inscription on his tombstone reads: GRAVE OF THE UNKNOWN PIG. That's all about to change.

"His name was Ted! We know that for sure now!" exclaimed an ecstatic devotee. She is just one of several thousand who have gathered here at graveside to share in the excitement, and pay homage to perhaps the greatest, but least known, pig of all time. It is not clear who or what he was to most of his cult followers: Where was he born? He *was* famous wasn't he? He'd have all the answers if he were here, wouldn't he? Did he find a cure? Did he topple a regime? Was he self-employed? Did he start an argument in bad company? Why was he taken from us? These are just a few of the many questions which remain unanswered.

Once completely shrouded in mystery, this simple grave attracts over 50,000 dedicated visitors annually. Most o them humbly approach the gravesite, stand, stare, weep shrug and walk away.

"We feel much closer to him now that we're on a first name basis. Now, all we have to do is crack his last name."

The unveiling of the new stone is scheduled to take place tomorrow at noon. I will be a magical and historical moment for these pigs. An undisclosed source within the Order of the Unknown Pig revealed to the Pig Times tha the new incription could be "TED BUT NOT FORGOTTEN" or "HONOR THE TED".

SAVE OUR BACON
Porkers Lobby Pope

Roman authorities have been beefing up security round the Vatican over the last week in anticipation of the massive gathering of hogs from around the world scheduled to assemble this Saturday (the Hebrew Sabbath).

The subject of discussion is the possibility of converting the entire Catholic Church (he largest church in the world) to Judaism. Organizers of the gathering said, "If we can convince the Catholics, other churches are sure to follow. This would reduce the consumption of pork dramatically."The Pontiff maintains, "Give us a person for the first seven years of his life and he'll always be Catholic."

Pigs protest, "Give a butcher a pig for twenty minutes and he'll turn him into anything you want!" They went on to say that pigs are in fact unclean and not suitable for human consumption.

READERS ENRAGED — No Section C

Readers of the Pig Times were enraged today when it was discovered that there was no Section C.

"Many of us," said a reader, "were looking forward to enjoying the **Better Holes In Gardens** column. Now we have to wait 'til tomorrow."

Section C was not available for comment.

No Story Continued

Continued from page 1

MISSING PIGS BULLETIN

If anyone can give any information leading to the whereabouts of the following pigs, PLEASE contact your local police station.

Missing since March, 1984

Missing since 1963

Disappeared June, 1979

Missing since August, 1981

DOCTORS SAY CURE FOR GREASY PIGS' DISEASE YEARS NOT DECADES AWAY

NEWARK (GP)—Doctors are now saying that a cure for the dreaded Greasy Pig's Disease is only a few short years away. Dr. Oscar Mayer said patients with the disease experience extremely greasy skin and a paranoid state in which they are convinced that someone is always trying to tackle them and put them upside down in a barrel. Dr. Mayer is the founder of the Dr. Oscar Mayer ~~packing house~~ Clinic for Greasy Pig's Disease.

IMPERSONATING AN OFFICER – Fulton Jailed

Slumpy Fulton was fined $250.00 and sentenced to serve two weeks in jail today for impersonating a police officer. "It's getting to the point where a pig can't even be himself anymore without getting arrested," barked an angry Fulton, protesting his innocence.

THE HEMLOCK SOCIETY ANNOUNCES LAST MEETING OF THE SEASON

The Hemlock Society will meet next Wednesday evening at 8 p.m. for the last time. A light lunch and beverage will be served.

Should you decide to wash... Tied in... Tied up!

S&M HOG EQUIPMENT WAREHOUSE

"It Hurts So Good"

We will not knowingly be overstocked

For "Your" Ears Only™
Tattooing outfit. Discomfort guaranteed. If this feels good, we'll give you your money back.
$29.95 Alphabet and numbers included

Keep your lover on hold with the OUCH™ **Brand Nose Noose**
Wonderfully painful. Delightfully inexpensive.
Only **$14.95**

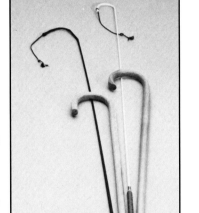

Or maybe you're into whips and canes
Whips made of genuine cowhide. Serves those cows right.
$12.00
Canes made of realistic wood.
Knock 'em silly for only **$9.95**

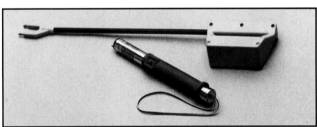

No! Not my big teeth you lunatic!
It's Doctor Snippers pearly strippers. Pliers manufactured from durable steel for the removal of your lovers' teeth against their will. Surprise them. Very kinky! Hurts like crazy.
$6.95

How about the Electric Shocker Prod?
This little persuader is great for poking fun at each other. She'll love it, he'll love it. Shocking results.
Only **$19.95** complete (batteries not excluded)

New Weaner Decks
You want out? You crawl over!
$89.95

Try to get out of this baby!
Introducing the Mach II Humiliation Confinement crate. It's an easily assembled, hot-dipped galvanized steel crate. You'll beg to get into it and plead to get out.
$119.95

S&M Hog Equipment Warehouse has the largest selection of painful – pleasureful – playthings. All items come fully guaranteed* or your money refunded.

*For as long as you live or for ten minutes, which ever comes first.

Order NOW
Call Toll Free **1-800-969-OUCH**
Ask for our catalogue of other fine products.